Shropshire Libraries	
67899	
PETERS	01-Aug-2019
J670	£12.99

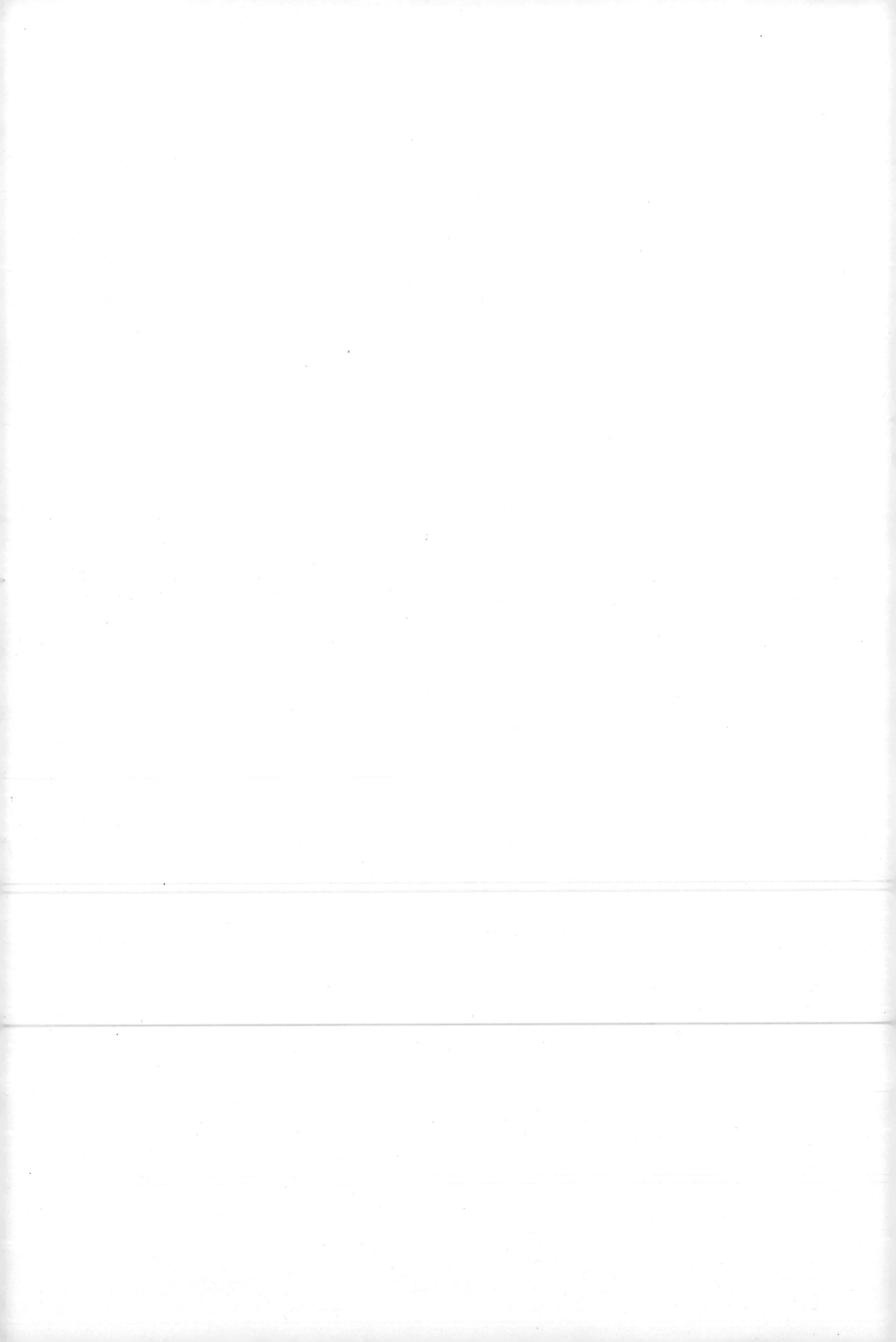

MATERIALS

BY
JOANNA BRUNDLE

©2017
Book Life
King's Lynn
Norfolk PE30 4LS

ISBN: 978-1-78637-210-9

All rights reserved
Printed in Malaysia

A catalogue record for this book
is available from the British Library.

Written by:
Joanna Brundle

Edited by:
Charlie Ogden

Designed by:
Drue Rintoul

Photocredits
Abbreviations: l-left, r-right, b-bottom, t-top, c-centre, m-middle.

Front Cover t – klublu. Front Cover mt – Songchai W. Front Cover mb – Songchai W. Front Cover b – photka. 1 – Alex Veresovich. 2 – Cyrustr. 4t – Billion Photos. 4bl – Theeradech Sanin. 4br – gmstockstudio. 5tr – LifetimeStock. 5b – 13Smile. 6tr – Eric Isselee. 6tl – Jerry Horbert. 6mr – optimarc. 6ml – Kyle Santee. 7tl – Sementer. 7tr – John Carnemolla. 7b – project1photography. 8tr – Surrphoto. 8b – Androlia. 9t – DimaSid. 9mr – designbydx. 9bl – Daniel Padavona. 10m – cozyta. 10br – stockphoto-graf. 11tl – Sakdinon Kadchiangsaen. 11b – George Burba. 12bl – Logutenko. 12br – Africa Studio. 13t – Lesterman. 13b – Melodia plus photos. 14b – yuratosno3. 15tr – Luba V Nel. 15m – ALEXANDER V EVSTAFYEV. 15b – Kjuuurs. 16l – doomu. 16bl – Dane-mo. 17t – Rob Hyrons. 17m – Africa Studio. 17b – DeymosHR. 18r – Rasulov. 18bl – Pefkos. 19tr – Love Silhouette. 19br – rng. 19ml – Fabio Pagani. 20tr – Gemenacom. 20bl – monticello. 21tl – Kekyalyaynen. 21b – Federico Rostagno. 22t – Nimit Ketkham. 22b – CREATISTA. 23tl – Jiri Vaclavek. 23b – S-Photo. 24tr – hxdyl. 24b – Grischa Georgiew. 25tr – Mega Pixel. 25b – Wara1982. 26tr – Dan Thornberg. 26b – tvist. 27tl – Garry0305. 27r – nuwatphoto. 27blt – Bjoern Wylezich. 27blm – Roman Bodnarchuk. 27bl – Zelenskaya. 28tr – Lyudmyla Kharlamova. 28bl – Everett Historical. 29t – Toa55. 29l – Mikhail Kolesnikov. 29b – John Gomez. 30t – O.Bellini. 30b – Andrey_Kuzmin. Images are courtesy of Shutterstock.com. With thanks to Getty Images, Thinkstock Photo and iStockphoto.

CONTENTS

Page 4 — WHAT ARE MATERIALS?
Page 6 — WHERE DO MATERIALS COME FROM?
Page 8 — CHOOSING AND USING MATERIALS
Page 10 — HOW CAN MATERIALS CHANGE?
Page 12 — MIXTURES AND SOLUTIONS
Page 14 — CHEMICAL CHANGES
Page 16 — CONDUCTORS AND MAGNETS
Page 18 — METALS
Page 20 — MAKING NEW MATERIALS – PLASTICS
Page 22 — MAKING NEW MATERIALS – GLASS
Page 24 — MAKING NEW MATERIALS – PAPER
Page 26 — DIFFERENT MATERIALS
Page 28 — IMPORTANT DISCOVERIES
Page 30 — EXPERIMENTS WITH MATERIALS
Page 31 — GLOSSARY
Page 32 — INDEX

Words that look like **this** are explained in the glossary on page 31.

WHAT ARE MATERIALS?

Materials are the things we use to make and build things. Take a look at the things around you now, such as this book, your desk, the building you are in and the clothes you are wearing. All of these things are made from materials.

SOLIDS, LIQUIDS AND GASES

All materials are made from **matter**. There are three different kinds of matter – solids, liquids and gases. These are called the three states of matter. A sugar cube is an example of a solid. Solids have a fixed shape. A sugar cube, like many solids, only changes its shape if you crush it. Solids have a fixed **volume**, meaning that they always take up the same amount of space.

Liquids, like this chocolate milk, can change shape. You can see this happening when you pour a drink from a bottle into a glass. The volume, however, stays the same.

Gases, such as steam from a kettle, have no fixed shape or volume. They float around and fill up the space they are in.

CHANGING STATES

Heating or cooling materials can change them from one state to another. If you put liquid water into a freezer, it turns into solid ice cubes. When you boil water in a kettle, some of it **evaporates** and turns into a gas – steam. Changes of state are **reversible**. When ice melts, it turns back into water. If steam hits a cold surface, it **condenses** and turns back into water.

WHAT IS MATTER MADE OF?

Around 2,500 years ago, an ancient Greek man called Democritus had the idea that a material cannot be cut into smaller and smaller pieces forever. He thought that, eventually, you would be left with a piece that was too small to cut in two. As it turns out, he was mostly right! All matter is made up of tiny, invisible **particles** called atoms. Atoms can join together to form groups called molecules.

The words we use to describe a material, such as 'hard' or 'stretchy', are its **properties**. A material's properties depend on how its atoms are arranged.

DID YOU KNOW? MOST MATERIALS CAN ONLY GO FROM A SOLID TO A GAS BY FIRST CHANGING INTO A LIQUID. **CARBON DIOXIDE** IS UNUSUAL BECAUSE IT CAN JUMP THE MIDDLE STEP. AT VERY LOW TEMPERATURES, CARBON DIOXIDE IS A SOLID. HOWEVER, IT CAN CHANGE INTO A GAS AND THEN GO BACK TO A SOLID, WITHOUT EVER BEING A LIQUID.

Atoms and molecules are held together by bonds. Solid materials, like diamond, are very hard because their atoms are held together with very strong bonds.

Glues are sticky because they contain molecules that can form strong bonds with the molecules in other substances.

The atoms and molecules in liquids have weaker bonds than solids. You can push your hand through water, but not through a lump of ice. Gases have no bonds. Their molecules move around freely.

WHERE DO MATERIALS COME FROM?

Some materials are **natural**. We get some natural materials from living things. Silk, for example, is taken from special insects called silkworms.

Silkworm

Many plants, like this cotton plant, provide us with natural materials.

Leather, wool and feathers are all examples of natural materials that we get from animals. Can you think of ways that we use these materials? Maybe you are wearing leather shoes or a woollen jumper right now!

Some natural materials, such as sand, granite and clay, do not come from living things. These are found on Earth or underground.

Granite Worktop

RENEWABLE AND NON-RENEWABLE MATERIALS

Some materials are renewable, meaning that they can be replaced. Trees can easily be planted to replace the trees that have been cut down for wood. This makes wood a renewable material.

Non-renewable materials cannot be replaced and will eventually run out. Non-renewable materials usually take millions of years to form, so we cannot quickly make or grow more. Non-renewable materials include **fossil fuels**, such as coal, oil and gas.

RAW MATERIALS

Raw materials, such as wood, rock and ore, are the main materials that we use to make things. An ore is a rock that contains a metal. An ore called bauxite contains the metal aluminium. Aluminium is used to make things that need to be light but strong, such as drinks cans.

A bauxite mine in Queensland, Australia.

Bauxite

Crude oil is a raw material that must be **refined**. It contains chains of molecules of different lengths called hydrocarbons. Refining crude oil sorts the hydrocarbons into similar sizes. This process produces many different materials, including petrol and diesel for cars, kerosene (aircraft fuel) and bitumen, a material used for building roads.

Oil rigs use long drills to reach pockets of crude oil that are buried deep underground.

CHOOSING AND USING MATERIALS

We can group materials together using their properties. Materials can be hard, soft, strong, weak, rough or smooth. Choosing the right material with the right properties is very important when making something.

LIFE AT HOME

Look at an object in your house. Why is it made from that material? If you have a slide in your garden, it is probably made from plastic. This is because plastic is waterproof and strong. Sofas are often made from wood and feathers. The wood makes the **frame** strong and the feathers make the cushions comfortable. A sofa made from **concrete** wouldn't be very comfortable at all!

In summer, we wear clothes made from thin, lightweight materials, such as cotton. In winter, we wear clothes made from materials that keep us warm, such as wool. Materials that stop heat from easily passing through them, like wool, are said to be good insulators.

Cotton

BUILDINGS AND CONSTRUCTION

It is important to use the right materials when constructing a building, because they need to stay standing for a long time, even in bad weather. Concrete and **steel** are often used when building large buildings, like skyscrapers, because they are very strong.

Bricks are used to build walls because they are strong and hard. Bricks are made from clay that has been baked in a special oven until it has become hard. Glass is used for windows because it is **transparent** and waterproof. Plastic is an ideal material for gutters and drainpipes because it doesn't rot and is **flexible**.

This bridge is being built using concrete and steel. Using strong materials will help the bridge to hold the weight of many vehicles.

MATERIALS IN SPORT

In many sports you need special clothing. The materials used in sports clothing often have properties that keep the sportsperson safe or help them to win.

American football players tackle hard! To protect their heads, they wear helmets made of hard, lightweight plastic. Strong, plastic-coated metal bars protect their faces. Transparent plastic visors protect their eyes, but still allow them to see clearly.

American Football Player

HOW CAN MATERIALS CHANGE?

Cutting, grinding and crushing are all examples of ways that materials can be changed. This type of change is called a physical change. Physical changes do not produce new materials. They change the shape and size of a material, but the original material is still there. Crushing drinks cans, crumpling paper bags and grating cheese are all examples of physical changes. What other examples can you think of?

A crushed can contains the same amount of aluminium as an uncrushed can. It just has a different shape.

Changes of state, like water freezing into ice, are also physical changes. When changes of state occur, the number of molecules in the material stays the same. Because the number of molecules stays the same, the weight of the material stays the same – ten grams of water freezes to make ten grams of ice.

NATURAL PROCESSES

Materials are often changed by natural processes. Weathering is an example of a natural process. Weathering is the process in which rocks are slowly worn away by the weather. Weathering can be caused by changes in temperature, strong winds, heavy rain and waves. Changes in temperature can make rocks **expand** and **contract** so that, eventually, cracks appear and pieces of rock break off.

NEW ROCKS

New rocks can take millions of years to form. Sedimentary rocks, such as sandstone and shale, form when small rocks and animal bones are buried and pressed together for a long time. When sedimentary rocks are squeezed together under very high temperatures, they can turn into another type of rock – metamorphic rock. This usually happens when sedimentary rocks are buried deep underground. Metamorphic rocks, such as slate, are usually harder and stronger than sedimentary rocks.

Sandstone

As this lava cools, it will become igneous rock.

Very high temperatures underground can melt rock into a liquid. This liquid is called magma when it is underground and lava when it is above ground. When volcanoes erupt, this liquid rock is forced to the surface. As it cools and hardens, it becomes the final type of rock – igneous rock.

MIXTURES AND SOLUTIONS

A 'mixture' is two or more substances that have been mixed together. If one substance **dissolves** into another, the mixture is called a solution. Sea water is a solution, as it is made up of water and dissolved salt. The substance that is dissolved – in this case, the salt – is called the solute. The substance that does the dissolving – in this case, the water – is called the solvent.

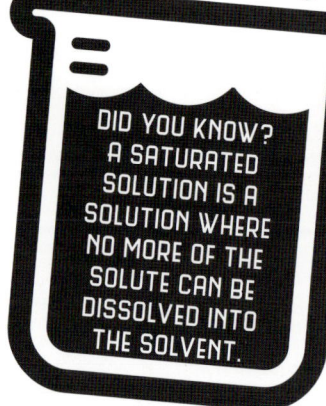

DID YOU KNOW? A SATURATED SOLUTION IS A SOLUTION WHERE NO MORE OF THE SOLUTE CAN BE DISSOLVED INTO THE SOLVENT.

SOLVENTS

Different solvents dissolve different things. Solvents that can dissolve stains on clothes are used in washing products. These solvents make the molecules in stains separate from one another so they can be washed off the clothing.

If you are cleaning paint brushes, you need to use the correct solvent for the type of paint you are using. Water will dissolve water-based paints, but oil-based paints have to be dissolved in a solvent called **turpentine**.

Cleaning Products

SEPARATING MATERIALS FROM MIXTURES

Particles that won't dissolve are called insoluble. Filtering is a process that removes insoluble particles from a liquid. When we strain vegetables and water through a sieve, we are filtering the mixture.

A solution cannot be separated by filtering or sieving. Tipping a bucket of salty seawater through a filter does not separate the salt and water! Instead, a solution can sometimes be heated so that the solvent evaporates and leaves the solute behind. The gas can then be condensed back into a liquid.

Sea salt and water can be separated through evaporation. This happens naturally when shallow pools of sea water, called salt pans, slowly evaporate in the sunshine. When this happens, sea salt gets left behind. In areas where there is not enough sunshine, indoor salt pans, which are heated by electricity, are used instead.

These salt pans are in the Canary Islands. The hot, dry weather is perfect for evaporating sea water.

CHEMICAL CHANGES

Chemical changes, which are also called chemical reactions, happen when the atoms in two different materials join together and make a new material. Things that chemically react with each other are called reactants. The new materials that are made are called products. Chemical changes are usually irreversible, which means that products cannot be changed back into reactants.

DID YOU KNOW? BAKING CAKES, FRYING EGGS, EXPLODING FIREWORKS AND SOURING MILK ARE ALL EXAMPLES OF IRREVERSIBLE CHEMICAL CHANGES. CAN YOU THINK OF SOME MORE?

COMBUSTION

Combustion is the scientific word for burning. It is a chemical change that takes place when a material reacts with **oxygen** at a very high temperature. Combustion gives off heat, as well as light and sound. Combustion shows us that the products of a chemical reaction sometimes have very different properties to the reactants that went into the reaction. Just think about how a bonfire looks when it is ready to be lit and how it looks after it has burned away.

REACTIVITY

A material's reactivity refers to how well it reacts with other materials. It is important to think about a material's reactivity before using it to make something. Jewellery, for example, is usually made from materials that do not react strongly with the oxygen in the air.

This ring is over 100 years old. It still looks good because it was made from a material with low reactivity.

Gold is often used to make jewellery. It stays shiny because it doesn't react with oxygen or water.

RUSTING

Rusting is a chemical reaction that happens when iron or steel reacts with oxygen. The chemical reaction that takes place makes a new substance called rust. The scientific name for rust is iron oxide.

The strong, hard steel used to build this boat has rusted into crumbly, weak iron oxide. Sea water speeds up rusting.

CONDUCTORS AND MAGNETS

Materials that allow electricity or heat to pass through them are called conductors. Materials that do not allow electricity or heat to pass through them are called insulators. We can sort materials into groups by how well they conduct heat or electricity. Some materials, such as copper, conduct both very well.

DID YOU KNOW? DIAMONDS CONDUCT HEAT BETTER THAN ANY OTHER MATERIAL.

HEAT CONDUCTORS

Metals are some of the best conductors of heat. When the atoms in conductors get hot, they **vibrate**. They pass on this heat energy to other atoms nearby, making them vibrate too. Plastic, wood and wool are poor conductors of heat.

DID YOU KNOW? GRAPHITE, WHICH IS USED INSIDE PENCILS, IS VERY UNUSUAL BECAUSE IT CAN CONDUCT ELECTRICITY EVEN THOUGH IT IS NOT A METAL.

The best metal for conducting heat is silver.

ELECTRICAL CONDUCTORS

Electrical conductivity is not the same as heat conductivity. Instead of the atoms vibrating, small parts of the atoms in electrical conductors can move around. In materials that are good electrical conductors, the particles that carry electricity, called electrons, move through the material taking the electricity with them. Most metals are very good electrical conductors. This is why electric fences are usually made from metal wire.

MAGNETS

We can also sort materials into groups using their magnetic properties – whether or not they can be pulled towards a magnet. Magnets produce an invisible force around them called a magnetic field. Magnetic objects are only affected by a magnet if they are inside its magnetic field. Some metals, such as iron and nickel, are magnetic. **Alloys** of these metals are also magnetic. Most other materials, including most other metals, are not magnetic.

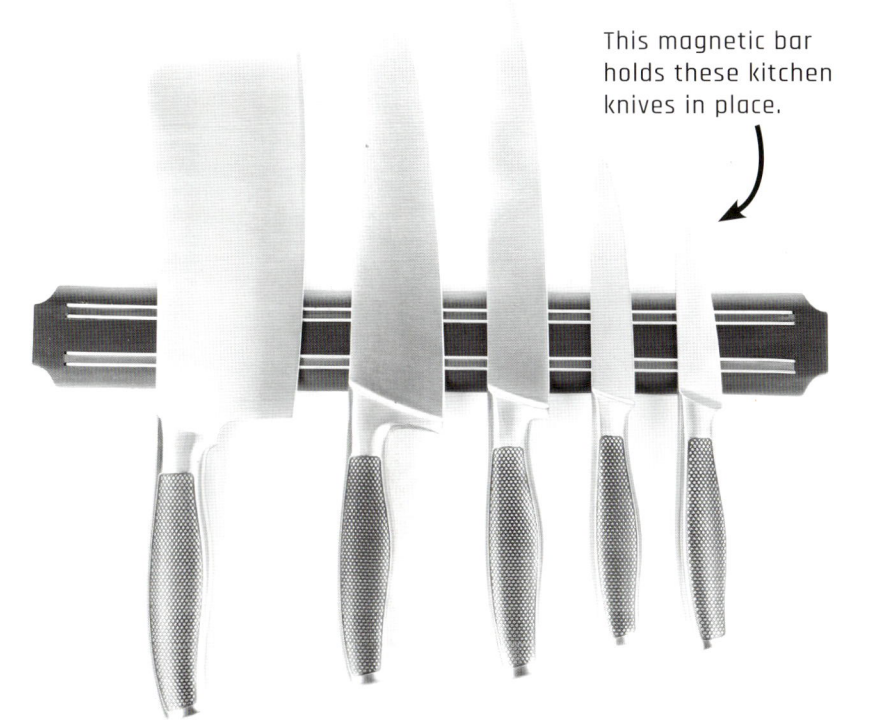

This magnetic bar holds these kitchen knives in place.

USES FOR MAGNETS

Magnets have many uses. They are often used in machines in hospitals as well as in the speakers in televisions, telephones and headphones. Vacuum cleaners use powerful magnets in their motors to make them suck up dirt. Magnets also hold your fridge and freezer doors closed.

Vending machines use magnets to make sure that only real coins are being used to buy things from them.

DID YOU KNOW? THE FIRST MAGNETS, CALLED LODESTONES, WERE STONES. THEIR MAGNETIC PROPERTIES WERE DISCOVERED OVER TWO THOUSAND YEARS AGO BY THE ANCIENT GREEKS.

METALS

Metals have many properties that make them useful. As we have seen, most metals are good conductors of heat and some are good conductors of electricity. Most metals only melt at high temperatures. Metals can also often be bent and shaped in order to make things, such as parts of cars. Metal alloys have different properties from the original metals that went into making them. For example, copper mixed with tin makes an alloy called bronze, which is stronger than both copper and tin.

FERROUS AND NON-FERROUS METALS

Ferrous metals, such as steel, are made of iron mixed with small amounts of other materials. Ferrous metals can be picked up by a magnet. Non-ferrous metals do not contain any iron and are usually not attracted to magnets.

DID YOU KNOW? THE BRONZE AGE, WHICH LASTED FROM 2500 BC TO 800 BC, BEGAN WHEN ANCIENT HUMANS MADE BRONZE IN THEIR CAMPFIRES. BRONZE WAS USED TO MAKE STRONG TOOLS, LIKE AXES.

COPPER

Copper is an extremely useful metal. It is ductile, which means that it can be hammered into a very thin sheet or stretched into very thin wires without breaking. It is also a good conductor of electricity. For these reasons, it is often used to make wires for electronic devices.

Gas and water pipes used to be made from copper because it didn't **corrode** and sections could be easily **welded** together. Copper pipes have now, however, been mostly replaced with plastic pipes. This is because copper is expensive and difficult to find, whereas plastic is cheap and easy to make.

Copper Wires

Copper also conducts heat well. Copper saucepans allow food to cook quickly.

Copper forms alloys very easily. As well as bronze, copper also makes an alloy called brass. Brass is a mixture of copper and another metal – zinc.

Brass is used to make musical instruments because it is easy to shape, but is also strong.

MAKING NEW MATERIALS PLASTICS

Plastics have many different uses. This is because they are waterproof, cheap to make and can easily be dyed different colours. Plastics go soft when they are heated. Because of this, they can be moulded into different shapes. Some plastics, such as polythene, are thin and flexible and can be used to make things like carrier bags. Other plastics, such as polystyrene, are stiff and bulky. You may have seen polystyrene used to protect things in parcels. Most plastics can be recycled.

These bottles, made from the plastic polypropylene, can be re-used or recycled.

WHERE DO PLASTICS COME FROM?

Have you ever wondered why the names of plastics often start with 'poly'? Well, 'poly' means 'many'. The names of plastics often start with 'poly' because plastics are made of lots of small molecules that are all joined together. Most plastics are made from chemicals that we get from oil.

This suitcase is made from polycarbonate, a strong, lightweight plastic.

DID YOU KNOW? PLASTICS CAN ALSO BE MADE FROM SOME NATURAL MATERIALS, INCLUDING WOOD AND EVEN BANANA SKINS!

HEATING PLASTICS

After plastic has been heated and moulded into shape, it cools and hardens. Some plastics can be heated and shaped many times. These are called thermo-plastics. PVC is a thermo-plastic and it is used to make toys, pipes and window frames.

Most window frames are now made from PVC rather than wood. This is because PVC can easily be moulded into any shape, is cheap and doesn't need to be painted.

DID YOU KNOW? PLASTIC COMES FROM THE GREEK WORD 'PLASTICOS', WHICH MEANS 'TO MOULD'.

Some plastics can only be heated and shaped once. These are called thermo-setting plastics. As they cool, they set into a shape and cannot be changed. A common example of this type of plastic is epoxy resin. It is able to bond firmly to other materials and it is waterproof. This makes it very useful for building boats.

MAKING NEW MATERIALS GLASS

Glass is not just used to make windows. Glass is in everything from computer screens to spectacles.

HOW IS GLASS MADE?

Glass is made by melting **minerals** together at very high temperatures. A mineral found in sand, called silica, is mixed with **limestone** and **soda ash**. The mixture is then heated to 1,700 degrees Celsius. The limestone makes the glass less likely to break. The soda ash lowers the temperature that the mixture needs to be heated at. This makes the process cheaper, because less energy is needed.

This silica sand is ready to be delivered to a glass factory.

Glass Blower

MOULDING GLASS

Once it has been heated, the mixture becomes soft. It can then be poured, pressed or moulded into different shapes. Glass can also be blown into different shapes by people called glass blowers. They dip a hollow tube, called a blow pipe, into the melted glass. The glass blower then blows down the tube to form a bubble of glass, which can then be shaped.

HISTORY OF GLASS MAKING

People have been making glass for thousands of years. Glass dating back to 4000 BC has been found. It was used to decorate stone beads. By 1500 BC, glass was being used to make containers, like drinking glasses. By the first century BC, glass blowing had been discovered and by the first century **AD**, clear glass was being made.

Obsidian

DID YOU KNOW? SOME VOLCANOES PRODUCE A NATURAL GLASS CALLED OBSIDIAN. IT IS MADE WHEN MOLTEN ROCK CONTAINING LARGE AMOUNTS OF SILICA COOLS VERY QUICKLY. OBSIDIAN WAS USED BY PEOPLE TENS OF THOUSANDS OF YEARS AGO TO MAKE ARROW HEADS AND BLADES.

LEAD CRYSTAL GLASS

Glass blowing sometimes made glass look cloudy rather than clear. Around 1675, a glass maker called George Ravenscroft discovered that, by adding **lead** to the mixture, he could make clear, sparkling glass. This became known as lead crystal glass and it was used to make spectacles and telescopes, as well as other things.

Lead Crystal Glass

MAKING NEW MATERIALS PAPER

To make paper, wood has to be chopped into very small pieces and then boiled with water and chemicals in order to make a slushy pulp. The water is then removed from the pulp to make it thicker.

The thick pulp is then squeezed between rollers, which removes more of the water. The rollers also make the paper pulp flat and smooth. Finally, it is pressed between heated rollers until it is completely dry.

FORESTRY

Trees are often specifically planted just so that their wood can be used to make paper. However, it takes a long time for trees to grow. Because of this, it is becoming more and more important that paper and paper products are recycled.

Paper

Waste Paper for Recycling

HISTORY OF PAPER MAKING

The word 'paper' comes from papyrus, a plant that was first used by the ancient Egyptians to make paper.

Paper as we know it was first produced in China in the first century AD. It was made from rags and a plant called bamboo. Following the invention of a wood grinding machine in the nineteenth century, wood became the main material used to make paper. During the twentieth century, machines started to be used to make paper. There are now lots of different types of paper, from sandpaper to wallpaper.

Most bank notes are made from paper, but some are now being made from plastic. These notes are cheaper to make and more hard-wearing than paper notes.

Paper made from the papyrus plant feels rough.

DIFFERENT MATERIALS

We have already seen that we can tell materials apart by how they react, conduct and behave around magnets. However, there are plenty more ways to tell materials apart.

DENSITIY

Density is a good way to sort materials into groups. Density describes how closely the molecules in a material are packed together. The more closely the molecules are packed, the denser the material is. Materials with high densities weigh more than materials with low densities. For something to be able to float, it must have a lower density than the material it is floating on.

The lightweight materials that life jackets are made from are much less dense than water. This is why they can help us to float.

Wood floats on water because it is less dense than water.

DID YOU KNOW?
THE DENSEST MATERIAL ON EARTH IS OSMIUM, A HARD METAL THAT IS OVER 20 TIMES DENSER THAN WATER. ONE OF THE LEAST DENSE MATERIALS IS A MAN-MADE MATERIAL CALLED AEROGRAPHITE. ALTHOUGH IT IS VERY LIGHT, IT CAN HOLD UP TO 40,000 TIMES ITS OWN WEIGHT! IT CAN POP BACK INTO SHAPE EVEN AFTER IT HAS BEEN SQUASHED AND CRUSHED.

MASS AND SIZE

A material's mass is the amount of matter that it is made from. However, looking at mass and size does not help us to tell materials apart.

A matchstick and a wooden table are very different in terms of mass and size. However, both are made from the same material – wood.

BOILING AND MELTING MATERIALS

Different materials change states at different temperatures. We can tell materials apart using these different temperatures. Water, for example, boils at 100 degrees Celsius and freezes at zero degrees Celsius.

The table below shows the melting points for some common metals. This information can be used to check whether a material is pure. If a material contains other metals, the melting point will be different.

METAL	MELTING POINT IN DEGREES CELSIUS
Silver	961.78
Gold	1063
Copper	1084.62

IMPORTANT DISCOVERIES

Some everyday materials were discovered by chance.

An American chemist, Spencer Silver, was trying to make a very sticky glue that could be used in aeroplanes and spacecraft, but he accidentally made a very weak glue instead. When it was stuck to a surface, this glue could be peeled away. It didn't damage the surface or leave any stickiness behind. Silver struggled to find a use for his material until a friend suggested sticking the glue to a piece of paper. The paper could then easily be stuck to anything else. And with that, the sticky note was born!

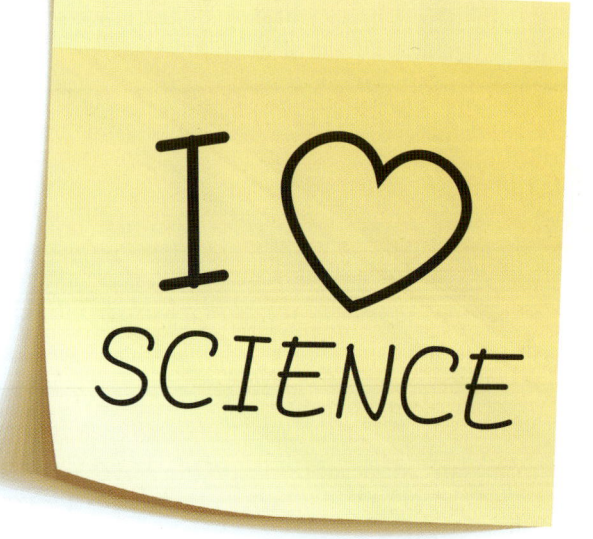

Sticky notes are used in homes and offices all over the world.

In 1839, American inventor Charles Goodyear accidentally discovered that heating liquid latex with sulphur made a strong, non-sticky rubber that could be used to make tyres. Latex is a sticky juice that comes from the rubber tree. Sulphur is a yellow, non-metallic material that is found in the ground.

Charles Goodyear

NOMEX

Firefighters need clothes made from a material that doesn't get damaged by fire. This is hard to come across, because most materials either burn or are not suitable for making clothes out of. The material that they use in their clothing is Nomex, a heat and flame resistant material that was invented by Wilfred Sweeny.

Nomex is used in the suits, helmets and gloves worn by firefighters. It is also found in the blankets used to protect people trapped by fire.

If racing cars crash, the fuel tanks can catch fire. Because of this, Nomex is used in the drivers' overalls, gloves, helmets and boots.

KEVLAR

Stephanie Kwolek was a scientist who worked for the same company as Wilfred Sweeny. In 1964, she discovered Kevlar. Kevlar is a type of plastic that can be woven into a strong, flexible and lightweight material. Kevlar is very hard to cut or break, so it is used in car and bicycle tyres.

Kevlar is also used to make bullet-proof vests.

EXPERIMENTS WITH MATERIALS

Look back to page 12 to remind yourself about saturated solutions. You can try making a saturated solution yourself by dissolving salt in water. Carefully measure out 100 millilitres of water and then add 35 grams of salt. Let the salt dissolve, then try adding more. What happens? You should find that the extra salt doesn't dissolve because the solution is saturated.

Mix some soil into a glass of water. It looks like you've made a solution by dissolving the soil into water, doesn't it? Now wait a few minutes and see what happens. You should find that the soil settles at the bottom of the glass. Why? Well, water is not a solvent for soil, so the soil can't dissolve into it. The soil is also denser than water, so it settles at the bottom of the glass.

Try comparing the density of water with the density of other materials by making a density tower. Very slowly and carefully, pour equal amounts of honey, milk, washing-up liquid, water and cooking oil into a glass one after the other. You should find they form five separate layers. They do this because each material has a different density.

GLOSSARY

AD	meaning 'in the year of the lord', it marks the year that Jesus was born and is used as the starting year for most calendars
alloys	mixtures of two or more chemical elements, of which at least one is a metal
BC	meaning 'before Christ', it is used to mark dates that occurred before the starting year of most calendars
carbon dioxide	a gas that occurs naturally in the atmosphere
concrete	a mixture of gravel, sand, cement and water used for building
condenses	changes from a gas to a liquid
contract	become smaller
corrode	wear or rot away by chemical action such as rusting
dissolves	mixes completely into a liquid to form a solution
evaporates	changes from a liquid to a gas
expand	become larger
flexible	able to bend without breaking
fossil fuels	fuels, such as coal, oil and gas, which formed millions of years ago from the remains of animals and plants
frame	the stiff structure that supports something
lead	a heavy, bluish-grey soft metal
limestone	a hard, chalky rock
matter	what everything is made from
minerals	natural, useful and sometimes valuable substances, often obtained from rocks underground
natural	not made by humans
oxygen	a colourless gas, needed by plants and animals to survive
particles	extremely small pieces of a substance
properties	the individual qualities of a material
refined	processed to give useful products
reversible	able to be undone or changed back
soda ash	a man-made and naturally occurring powdery compound
steel	a hard, strong, grey alloy of iron and other substances
transparent	allowing light to pass through
turpentine	a strong-smelling oily solvent used for mixing paint and cleaning brushes
vibrate	move quickly left and right, backwards and forwards or up and down
volume	the amount of space that a quantity of a substance takes up
welded	heated to melting point, then pressed or hammered together

INDEX

A
alloys 17-19
atoms 5, 14, 16

B
bonds 5

C
carbon dioxide 5
changes
-chemical 14
-irreversible 14
-physical 10
-reversible 5, 14
combustion 14
condensation 5
conductors 16, 18

D
Democritus 5
density 26, 30

E
electricity 13, 16, 18-19
evaporation 13

F
fuels
-fossil 6

G
gases 4-5
glass 4, 9, 22-23, 30
Goodyear, Charles 28

H
hydrocarbons 7

K
Kwolek, Stephanie 29

L
liquids 4, 5

M
magnets 16-18, 26
mass 27
matter 27
-states of 4-5
metals 16-18, 27
-ferrous 18
-non-ferrous 18
minerals 22
mixtures 12-13, 19, 22-23
molecules 5, 7, 10, 12, 20, 26

N
non-renewables 6

O
obsidian 23
oil 7, 12, 20, 30
-crude 7
osmium 26
oxygen 14, 15

P
paper 10, 24-25, 28
particles 5, 13, 16
plastics 8-9, 16, 19-21, 25, 29
products 12, 14, 24
properties 5, 8-9, 14, 17, 18

R
Ravenscroft, George 23
reactants 14
reactions
-chemical 14-15
reactivity 15
renewables 6
rocks
-igneous 11
-metamorphic 11
-sedimentary 11

S
Silver, Spencer 28
solids 4, 5
solutes 12
solutions 12-13, 20
-saturated 12, 30
solvents 12-13, 30
Sweeny, Wilfred 29

V
volume 4